LONDON'S
UNDERGROUND
PAST
and
PRESENT

THE CENTRAL LINE

The Central Line

LONDON'S
UNDERGROUND
PAST
and
PRESENT

THE CENTRAL LINE

ROBERT GRIFFITHS

Past & Present Publishing Ltd

First published in 2007

British Library Cataloguing in Publication Data

A catalogue record for this book is available from the British Library.

ISBN 978 1 85895 217 8

Past & Present Publishing Ltd
The Trundle
Ringstead Road
Great Addington
Kettering
Northants NN14 4BW

Tel/Fax: 01536 330588
email: sales@nostalgiacollection.com
Website: www.nostalgiacollection.com

Printed and bound in the Czech Republic

CONTENTS

Left Harry C. Beck was an engineering draughtsman at the London Underground Signals Office, and in his spare time he designed the diagram of the London Underground tube map. He laid out his maps geographically, often superimposed on a road map. When he left London Transport he taught typographics and colour design at the London School of Printing and Kindred Trades, but will always be known as the tube map designer. He died in 1974 and in the early 1990s the London Transport Museum created the Beck Gallery, and a commemorative plaque was put up at Finchley Central tube station.

Over the years the Underground map has seen many alterations, with the closing and opening of lines and stations. This photograph shows a map of the Central London Railway, which ran from Wood Lane to Liverpool Street, and has certainly seen many changes, including the re-naming of some stations; for example, Queens Road became Queensway, and Post Office became St Paul's. Interchange stations were later added, and finally the Central Line was extended to Ongar and West Ruislip.

There are thousands of maps on the London Underground, ranging from large wall maps displayed on stations to pocket maps, free to the passengers and obtainable from booking offices. In addition each line displays its own station list in both directions on station walls and inside every carriage, and modern automated voice announcements make it very hard for anyone to get lost on the London Underground today! *John Glover*

NORTHOLT: The 'past' photograph, taken on 16 May 1955, shows a smart ticket collector standing in his box, while on the right can be seen the booking office window. This temporary booking hall was replaced by a permanent structure later on.

The recent photograph shows how vast improvements have been made to the Underground to keep up with modern technology. *London Transport Museum/RG*

INTRODUCTION

The Central London Railway opened on 30 July 1900. Wood Lane depot served the line, running the early type of tube stock from Shepherds Bush to Bank. The depot consisted of a power station, carriage sheds and carriage repair shops, encircled by a loop line. Today the depot is gradually being demolished to make room for a shopping centre, and a new depot, consisting of 16 carriage roads, is being built underground.

The line was extended to Ealing Broadway on 3 August 1920, and East, North and West Acton stations were built to offer a frequent service for the many passengers who preferred to use the tube rather than the motor buses; the latter were slow, some companies were more expensive than others and the winter months made travelling by road uncomfortable.

By 1912 the line had been extended from Bank to Liverpool Street, and the company ordered more stock to operate the line as passenger numbers increased, taking advantage of the fast and cheap journeys – the Central London became known as the 'Twopenny Tube'. By 1933 British Museum station had closed, with Holborn (Kingsway) station having been built east of the Museum; Holborn became a very busy interchange for the Piccadilly Line. In July of the same year the London Passenger Transport Board was formed, although it did not come into force legally until 10 March 1939.

More tunnelling work from Liverpool Street to Stratford led to a further extension, which opened 4 December 1946. A fan shaft for evacuation purposes was built between Mile End and Stratford, known as the Old Ford fan shaft, as the distance between the two stations was 2.83km.

The war years held up much of the proposed work on the Central Line, with train services interrupted by air-raids and people using the Underground stations as shelters to escape the falling bombs and 'doodlebugs' that caused so much damage to London. Part of the new Leytonstone-Newbury Park extension, between Wanstead and Redbridge, was used as a factory for aeroplane parts before opening through to Hainault on 31 May 1948. By the end of that year services were operating from Hainault to Woodford, and Leytonstone to Loughton, using standard tube stock based at Hainault to serve the east end of the line; sidings for stabling trains overnight at Woodford and Loughton are used to this day. Hainault depot consists of carriage sheds, workshops and a train-wash through which drivers have to take their trains when stabling them on the many carriage roads, north or south of the depot. The depot can be entered from both Hainault and Grange Hill, which is ideal for London-bound trains running via either Newbury Park or Woodford.

Also by 1948 the west end of the line had been extended to West Ruislip, and the depot built there stretched from Ruislip Gardens station to West Ruislip, a distance of 2.04km; it consisted of workshops, carriage sheds, train-wash and many long carriage roads. Trains can enter and leave the depot from both ends, and it is also used for the transfer of rolling-stock and equipment.

The Great Eastern Railway, subsequently the Eastern Region of British Railways, had run steam trains from Ongar to Liverpool Street since 1865, then London Transport took over the line from 1948 as part of the central Line. Because they had been built in Victorian days, most stations still featured the 'GER' monogram in the ironwork of the station canopy supports. Some with the original wooden canopies and station buildings have hardly changed, except for the ticket barriers and improved lighting. The stations from Ongar to Leyton had their own sidings or goods yards for coal supplies until every goods yard eventually became a car park. For safety reasons, since the line now had live rails for the electric tube trains, footbridges and road bridges replaced level crossings. Meanwhile more housing and factories were being built along the line, giving the Central Line increasing passengers numbers each year. Timetables were rewritten as more trains were put into service to cope with the rush-hours, and a special timetable was introduced for late-night shopping in London on Thursdays.

In 1957 London Transport also took over the Epping to Ongar line, following the sad farewell journey of the last steam train. Four-car tube trains were used to operate a shuttle service between Epping and Ongar until the line closed on 30 September 1994. It has since been taken over by Epping Ongar Railway Ltd, running a Sunday service to Coopersale and attracting visitors to admire their old rolling-stock and steam locomotives on show at Ongar. Blake Hall station is now a private house with its single-line platform removed.

Since 1994 the Central Line 1962 tube stock, which was operated by a driver and guard, has been taken away for scrap, replaced by one-man-operated 1992 tube stock. Some tunnel sections had to be widened and block marker boards took the place of many colour light signals for ATP (automatic train protection) and ATO (automatic train operation). All the signal cabins closed, with signals and points operated from Wood Lane Control Centre near Shepherds Bush. Train and depot staff undertook extensive training to learn how to cope with the new stock, how to maintain it and correct any faults. The Central Line suffered teething troubles in the first few months until they were all sorted out to provide a decent and reliable train service.

The Central Line is currently undergoing a refurbishment programme for track and stations that will certainly make it better in every respect and more comfortable for passengers, despite some of its 49 stations having to be closed for a period of time and track renewal work along its 46 miles being carried out at weekends.

In September 2006 the Central Line was named the best rail link in London at the National Rail Awards. It carries some 600,000 passengers per day, and has continued to improved its service over the past few years.

ACKNOWLEDGEMENTS

With 40 years of service on the Central Line, this book has arisen from my knowledge of and interest in the London Underground. I would like to thank John Glover, Brian Morrison, David Henderson, Jim Wright, Aidan Kelly, Bob Yeldham, John Carter, Alan Richards, Alan Rawling, Epping Forest District Museum and London Transport Museum for helping to make the book possible by providing the 'past' photographs from their collections. A special thanks goes to Malcolm Hills, Chairman and Operations Manager of the Epping Ongar Railway, which has brought back to life the branch line since its closure in September 1994.

ONGAR TO EPPING

In 1856 The Eastern Counties Railway opened a double-track railway between Stratford and Loughton, with a single-track extension from Loughton to Ongar added in 1865. Later this became part of the Great Eastern Railway. Plans to extend the line to Dunmow never saw the light of day.

The London Transport Board, established in 1933, and the main-line railway company got together with the aim of electrifying the line, hoping to reduce costs and provide an improved service. This scheme went ahead and the Central Line was extended to Ongar in 1957, at which time it was electrified and double track introduced between Loughton and Epping.

Blake Hall station closed on 31 October 1981 due to falling passenger numbers, and gradually, with a decline in passengers using Ongar and North Weald, the line closed altogether on 30 September 1994. The many memories shared by staff and passengers included the rabbit that jumped into the cab and bit the train driver, and the scorpions found on Ongar platform, which made the TV news and national newspapers!

Almost ten years to the day after the line closed, the first Epping Ongar Railway Volunteer Society train left Ongar at 11.00am on 10 October 2004, to introduce an hourly passenger service to North Weald on summer Sundays. Volunteers gradually restored the line and the station buildings that had become neglected over the previous ten years, and extra track was laid at Ongar to accommodate nostalgic rolling-stock, including steam locomotives from Finland.

ONGAR: A Holden 'F5' 2-4-2T builds up steam on 9 November 1957 to begin its return journey to Stratford, a few days before the last steam locomotive was to be replaced by standard tube stock on the electrification of the line on 18 November. *Covey Crumps*

ONGAR: The same 'F5' is seen from a different angle on the same day.

Following the withdrawal of steam the 1962 tube stock became a familiar sight on the Ongar line, operating what was known as the Ongar shuttle; four carriages only were used because of the length of the platforms. Eventually Craven 1960 tube stock was used in one-man-operated mode to serve until the closure of the line on 30 November 1994. This photograph was taken on the trackside on the last day.

Ten years later the line was re-opened by the Epping Ongar Railway Volunteer Society, the support group of the operating company, Epping Ongar Railway Ltd. This photograph was taken on 23 July 2006, and shows the locomotives from Finland on display beside the DMU, which is getting ready for its return journey to North Weald in passenger service. The unit has reversed at Coopersale, further up the line; although there is no station, the scenery of fields and forest along the 6-mile route in the heart of the Essex countryside is breathtaking.
Covey Crumps/J. Wright/RG

ONGAR: Looking in the opposite direction on a peaceful day in January 1990, a train of 1962 tube stock awaits its return journey to Epping. These trains were crewed by a driver and guard, and were stabled at Loughton sidings.

Once again, the DMU stands in its place, and bringing back something of the pre-tube-train nostalgia is the old rolling-stock beside it on display. *David Henderson/RG*

BLAKE HALL: The first two photographs were taken in 1956, with a Holden 'F5' pulling just two coaches because of the short platforms here and at North Weald. The station was built in 1865 with a staff dwelling and a small booking office. It was always the least used by passengers on the entire network, notching up about six per day!

When the station closed in October 1981 the platform was demolished and the station building sold; it is now a private dwelling. The second and third photographs were taken from the road bridge, looking towards North Weald. *Peter J. G. Pearson/ Covey Crumps/RG*

BLAKE HALL: An Essex country station surrounded by fields with very few dwellings nearby, Blake Hall is an unusual survivor, and the new owners have made the station an elegant home – no one could fail to give them full credit for the work that has been carried out. The 'past' photograph was taken in 1956 – it looks very peaceful, without a person or vehicle in sight, certainly proving how quiet this station was. *Peter J. G. Pearson/RG*

NORTH WEALD: The Ongar line has certainly seen some different types of rolling-stock in its time. This undated photograph captures a train of 1935 tube stock, and shows the passing loop at North Weald before Platform 1 closed in 1976; the track was subsequently lifted and the signal cabin taken out of commission, with Epping signal cabin operating the signals for Ongar and North Weald.

The station buildings have hardly change in the intervening years. The EOR DMU arrives at North Weald, passing the disused waiting room and signal box and empty trackbed on the left. *Bob Sheen/RG*

NORTH WEALD: The Holden 'F5s' were used regularly on the Epping to Ongar line, and here we see No 67218 on the left and No 67200 on the right in a busy scene from the 1950s.

The boarded-up signal box is seen again on the right, which I believe the Epping Ongar Railway will restore in time. Personally, I would like to see the passing loop replaced or another track placed beside the platform and used as a siding, to restore the former appearance of the station. *Covey Crumps/RG*

EPPING: The fireman fills the tank of Holden 'F5' 2-4-2T No 67200 before it continues its journey to Ongar on 9 November 1957. The water tower was sited on the opposite, eastern, side of the station, on the end of the platform where a train of London Transport standard tube stock awaits its journey to West Ruislip or Ealing Broadway.

Despite the introduction of tube trains, the station has kept its former appearance, except for modern lighting, CCTV cameras and the newly paved platforms, as it undergoes refurbishment in 2006. *Covey Crumps/RG*

EPPING: Central Line trains terminated at Epping, connecting with the Ongar shuttle until the line onward closed in 1994; passengers had to cross the footbridge to board the shuttle (on the left) and continue their journey. The first photograph was taken from the footbridge in January 1990.

Platform 2 is still used for the regular service to and from London, and I have heard a few passengers complain about still having to cross the footbridge, especially in bad weather conditions or when carrying heavy luggage. At least they have an excellent train service and wait no more than 10 minutes for their train. *David Henderson/RG*

EPPING TO WEST RUISLIP
AND EALING BROADWAY

EPPING: This view from the early days of steam shows the signal box on Platform 2, from which the signalman had easy views of the platforms and goods yard. Before London Transport took over the line in 1947 a new signal cabin was built further down the line. This closed on 28 July 1996 and all signal and point operation was taken over by Loughton signal cabin until it was transferred to Wood Lane signal control centre. *Epping Forest District Museum/RG*

EPPING LOCO SHED: The shed included a 50-foot turntable, used mainly by the 'J15' 0-6-0s that generally worked the goods trains – Nos 65444 and 65449 are seen on 8 August 1953. The tank engine on the right is Class 'C12' No 67363, which was converted for 'push-pull' operation but only stayed for a short time. Goods trains worked to Temple Mills and Ongar, and Epping also had a coal yard, which kept it very busy.

The shed and goods yard were demolished in the 1960s and London Transport turned the site into a car park; Epping's population was growing and extra space was needed for passengers to park their vehicles. With 6,200 passengers per day using Epping station and only 508 car-parking spaces, there are plans to extend the parking to another level. *Brian Morrison/RG*

THEYDON BOIS station was called simply 'Theydon' when opened by the Great Eastern Railway (GER) on 24 April 1865. It was renamed 'Theydon Bois' in December 1865, and Central Line trains served the station from 25 September 1949.

With daily use by no more than 1,600 passengers, Theydon Bois is still classed as a quiet station, especially on Sundays, unless visitors use it for walks to Epping Forest. *Epping Forest District Museum/RG*

DEBDEN was also opened on 24 April 1865 as part of the extension of the GER branch from Loughton to Ongar. Originally named 'Chigwell Road', it was renamed 'Chigwell Lane' on 1 December 1865, then became Debden on 25 September 1949 when the line was transferred to London Transport. The 'past' photograph shows a train of 1960 tube stock arriving at the westbound platform on 20 June 1961.

The recent photograph shows how much refurbishment has taken place at the station without changing its appearance from its early days; a train of 1992 tube stock, which runs automatically, is arriving at the westbound platform. Trains can reverse here using the crossover at the east end of the platforms, which replaced two sidings in the 1990s. *London Transport Museum/RG*

LOUGHTON opened on 22 August 1856 as the terminus of a branch line from London. The first station was sited in the vicinity in Loughton High Road near Lopping Hall, its exact location unknown. By the 1920s a new station had been built further south, with a goods yard and sidings.

In 1940 it was decided to re-site the station once again for the final time, with approval from the local council and the London & North Eastern Railway (LNER), successor to the GER. When London Transport took over in 1949 the station was also used as a train depot for train crews, LT providing ten sidings. When the company plan came into force in the early 1990s Loughton train crews were transferred to Hainault and Leytonstone to save the company money, although trains operated by Leytonstone train crews still use the ten sidings. It was decided to re-open Loughton for train crews once again in November 2006, and the old sub-station was refurbished for use as crew facilities and offices.
Epping Forest District Museum/RG

BUCKHURST HILL also opened on 22 August 1856. Its typical Victorian station building, built to last, has served many passengers each day throughout its history from steam to tube trains. The goods station, located at Queens Road, was opened in 1859 and closed on 6 January 1964. This photograph was taken in 1905.

The present-day view shows the splendour of the station. The platforms are at a lower level, with original waiting rooms. However, the goods yard has been transformed into a car park. *Epping Forest District Museum/RG*

BUCKHURST HILL: This photograph shows the original station of 1856, which had staggered platforms. The station building survives as a residence and offices to the south of the present platforms, the entrance having been moved to Victoria Road, and part of the original platform can also be seen. *Epping Forest District Museum/RG*

WOODFORD: The Craven 1960 tube stock was used as a shuttle for the Woodford to Hainault line from April 1964. The trains were later converted to automatic – driver only – as an experiment in advance of the automatic working of the Victoria Line, which opened in stages from 1968 to 1971. This photograph was taken in the mid-1970s.

When the 1992 stock was introduced to the line in 1994, it took over the Hainault to Woodford line, running a through service from West Ruislip and Ealing Broadway round the loop line, although still reversing at Woodford, except for trains that started service from Hainault depot via Grange Hill. *J. Wright/RG*

SOUTH WOODFORD: This early photograph, taken in August 1935, displays the name 'George Lane' on the building. This was changed to South Woodford in 1937 by the LNER. There is no longer access to the footbridge from the road that once crossed the line by a level crossing, which was removed when London Transport took over.

The recent photograph shows how much the station has been refurbished over the years, although it still retains the old-style waiting rooms on the platforms and the wooden canopy. Although the station was renamed, the London Underground roundels still display 'George Lane' beneath the station name. *London Transport Museum/RG*

SNARESBROOK: In the days of steam Snaresbrook station certainly presents a fine picture complete with signal box and semaphore signals, and bay platform and sidings on the left, which were all removed when London Underground took over in 1947.

The recent photograph taken from a Central Line train driving cab during a journey to Epping shows the block marker board signal for automatic working on the left and freshly laid ballast after track replacement on the eastbound line. *Bob Yeldham collection/RG*

LEYTONSTONE: Due to a derailment at Chancery Lane on 25 January 2003, caused by a gearbox failure, the Central Line was closed for a few months while all trains were inspected for safety reasons. Every station became a ghost station as Central Line passengers used alternative routes for their journeys, mainly buses or main-line railways. This unusual photograph was taken during the afternoon when the station was normally busy, but it is completely deserted. In due course the Central Line began to run again normally and safely. *RG*

BETWEEN LEYTONSTONE AND LEYTON: As well as vast changes over the years in tube stock and stations, changes can also be noted between stations with new signalling, buildings and vegetation on either side of the railway track. The first photograph, taken in 1983, shows an old colour light signal, now replaced by a block marker board for automatic working. The left-hand side of the track was once lined by terraced houses, but these were demolished to make room for the A12 Eastway, which caused so much protest in the 1990s. Old-style footbridges, such as that in the distance, were removed and replaced with glass-covered walkways. *J. Carter/RG*

LEYTON: The Great Eastern Railway opened a new signal box here in 1899. When London Transport took over the line in 1947 Leyton became a junction, because by then the Central Line's tunnel section from Liverpool Street to Leyton had been completed, and the signal box had to be moved back a few inches to make room for the new tracks.

By the late 1990s the signal box was demolished, the junction having already been removed a few years earlier. On the left-hand side of the 'present' photograph is the A12 Eastway instead of GER tracks. *J. Wright/RG*

STRATFORD: Looking westbound toward the tunnel section in 1973, the disused platform on the right was later used by the Docklands Light Railway (DLR), work on which began in 1984. The line was completed in July 1987 and officially opened by Queen Elizabeth II. The trains are fully automatic and operated entirely by an onboard computer system linked to a central control room. The Passenger Service Agent, whose job is to check tickets, make announcements and operate the doors, takes over control if there are any problems.

Stratford station is also served by the national rail network and the Jubilee Line, making it a very busy interchange. Vast improvements are being made for the 2012 Olympic Games at Stratford. A new station for the DLR is being built on the left-hand side of the Central Line, which will have two platforms and be better for passengers. The upgraded complex will have two new entrances and 14 lifts. *J. Wright/RG*

MILE END station was opened in 1902 by the Whitechapel & Bow Railway, and electrified services started in 1905. In 1912 ownership passed to the Midland Railway, and in 1923 the London, Midland & Scottish Railway (LMS), with services also operated by the District Line with the Hammersmith & City Line. The Metropolitan Line followed in 1936.

The station was rebuilt and expanded in 1946 as part of the Central Line's eastern extension, with services beginning on 4 December. With the nationalisation of the railways in 1948 the station passed to London Underground. This is the only subterranean station on the network that offers cross-platform interchange between the 'tube' (tunnelled) and 'cut and cover' (excavated and roofed-over) lines of the Central and the District/Hammersmith & City lines. When photographed the station was undergoing refurbishment to brighten up the dimly lit platforms and upgrade the interior to the improved standard of the modern tube network. *London Transport Museum/RG*

BETHNAL GREEN: This station is a fine and typical example of the 'New Works Programme' of 1935-40, with its pale yellow tiling manufactured by Poole Pottery. The 'past' photograph, taken on 2 January 1947, shows a train of standard tube stock waiting in the eastbound platform, with fluorescent lighting suspended from the tunnel roof. The station is supposed to be haunted. During the Second World War the air-raid warning sounded, causing panic, and as the crowd surged forward a woman tripped on the stairs, causing many others to fall. Three hundred people were crushed in the tiny stairwell – 172 people were dead and more died later in hospital later; 69 of the dead were children.

The recent photograph shows 1992 tube stock and the station undergoing refurbishment. All the yellow tiles are being replaced, and modern lighting and station equipment installed. *London Transport Museum/RG*

LIVERPOOL STREET is a major London railway station, opened on 2 February 1874 by the Great Eastern Railway. Deep-level tube platforms were opened on 28 July 1912 by the Central London Railway, and at the time this was the end of the line until it was extended eastwards on 4 December 1946 as part of the war-delayed London Passenger Transport Board's 'New Works Programme'. The 'past' photograph was taken on 16 May 1923 looking along Broad Street, showing the entrance to the Central, Metropolitan, Hammersmith & City and Circle underground lines in front of the former North London Railway's Broad Street terminus on the right.

In 1985-91 the main-line station was extensively redeveloped, and today the new station entrance is on the left of the photograph, while offices stand on the original site. *London Transport Museum/RG*

BANK station certainly needed a coat of paint judging from this photograph taken on 6 April 1984. The sharply curved track from Liverpool Street to St Paul's and the curved platform at Bank station were built to avoid the bank vaults of the Bank of England.

Today the station is very busy with interchanges for the Northern and Waterloo & City underground lines and the Docklands Light Railway. In the 1990s it was refurbished with improved lighting and tiling, which certainly changed its appearance. *J. Glover/RG*

BANK: A train of 1962 stock arrives at the eastbound platform in the early 1990s, since replaced by 1992 stock. The station had been refurbished by this time – note the new train describer and signs. An automatic public address system was installed that advised passengers to 'Mind the gap' every time a train arrived in the platform. Before that a member of staff had to stand on the platform shouting out the warning, and giving the 'right away' to the guard when it was safe for the train doors to close. *J. Glover/RG*

ST PAUL'S station opened on 30 July 1900 as 'Post Office', after the headquarters of the General Post Office on St Martin's le Grand. When the station was modernised in the 1930s its entrance was located on the north side of Newgate Street, but was later moved to the east, and an office block built in its place. A modern ventilation shaft in the centre of the traffic island at the junction indicates the location of the original lift shafts. The station received its present name after the other St Paul's station was renamed Blackfriars in 1937.

At the time of writing the platforms look very dismal, because of refurbishment work being carried out under the Central Line modernisation scheme. *London Transport Museum/RG*

CHANCERY LANE, which had 'Grays Inn' added to its name in 1934, had been closed to passengers on Sundays for many years until 2006, when it was allowed to remain open. The 'past' photograph, taken on 21 July 1934, shows the escalators, 'passimeter' booking office and ticket machines that were a common sight at that time.

The Underground network has improved over the years with new ticket machines and barriers – passengers and staff can feel proud of their modern newly refurbished station. *London Transport Museum/RG*

HOLBORN is the interchange between the Central Line and the Piccadilly Line, which was opened by the Great Northern, Piccadilly & Brompton Railway (GNP&BR) on 15 December 1906 with the name Holborn (Kingsway). There was no interchange with the Central Line until 25 September 1933 – the nearest Central Line station had previously been British Museum, which closed when new interchange facilities were brought into use at Holborn. The 'past' photograph was taken on 12 May 1954, and shows the London Transport signs that have now been replaced with Underground ones – but the newspaper seller still stands in the same place! *London Transport Museum/RG*

TOTTENHAM COURT ROAD: In July 1988 an eastbound train of 1962 stock arrives at the busy platform that serves as an interchange with the Northern Line. Modernisation of the station began in February 1986 and was completed in May 1992 with mosaic tiles, new escalators, and a large new ticket hall.

The 'present' photograph was taken in May 2007, with no passengers in sight. Only a member of the station staff can be seen, ensuring that the platforms are empty after the departure of the last train of the day some 10 minutes before. *J. Glover/RG*

OXFORD CIRCUS is the interchange for the Bakerloo and Victoria lines. Since the latter opened on 7 March 1969 the station has become extremely busy, although it was already one of the busiest on the Central Line, with Oxford Street always packed with shoppers and tourists. This station was recognised by its 'snakes and ladders' mosaic tiling, as shown in the photograph of the westbound platform taken in April 1984.

The station is currently undergoing a major modernisation – the mosaic tiles are being replaced by white tiles and many more improvements will take place. The second photograph was taken late at night in May 2007, capturing just three passengers, a very rare sight at this busy station. *J. Glover/RG*

BOND STREET was opened by the Central London Railway on 24 September 1900, and the building was designed by the architect Harry Bell Measures. Several major reconstructions saw the original lifts replaced by escalators and a new sub-surface ticket hall and street-level facade. In 1980 all was demolished with the construction of the new 'West One' shopping arcade, which is now the entrance to the station. The Jubilee Line opened on 1 May 1979, giving the Central Line another interchange station. The 'past' photograph shows the westbound Central Line platform on 23 August 1973 – a typical 1970s platform with clock and train describer under dim lights, compared with the present photograph of the platform from the same position. *London Transport Museum/RG*

MARBLE ARCH: The 'past' photograph was taken on 21 October 1924, and shows the original station on the corner of Oxford Street and Quebec Street. This station was served by lifts to the platforms, but was reconstructed in the early 1930s to accommodate escalators, at which time the original station entrance was closed and later demolished. A replacement sub-surface ticket hall opened further to the west. *London Transport Museum/RG*

Right From Ward Lock's *London*, 1910.

OXFORD STREET AND HOLBORN.

ROUTE VI.—OXFORD STREET—SOHO—TOTTENHAM COURT ROAD—BLOOMS-BURY—THE BRITISH MUSEUM—HOLBORN.

We will assume this time that the start is made from **Oxford Circus**, at the junction of Oxford Street with Regent Street.

Oxford Street.

Plan II. H. and I. 7.
Stations, commencing at west end, Marble Arch, Bond Street, Oxford Circus, Tottenham Court Road and British Museum. All these are on the Central London Tube. At Oxford Circus connection is made with the Bakerloo Tube, at Tottenham Court Road with the Hampstead Tube, and the British Museum station is quite close to the Holborn station of the Piccadilly Tube.

This has always been the principal traffic artery between the west and north-west of London and the City. The opening of the Central London Railway, or "Tube," in 1900, so far from displacing the 'buses, only led to an increase in their numbers. Although Oxford Street proper, from the Marble Arch to Tottenham Court Road, has only a length of a mile, it forms part of a great highway extending from the Bank to Shepherd's Bush, and thence viâ Acton and Ealing to Uxbridge. At and near Oxford Circus are some of the best known shops in London, including *Marshall and Snelgrove's*, *Peter Robinson's*, *Jay's*, *Selfridge's*, *Liberty's*, *Dickens and Jones's*, *D. H. Evans'*, *Waring's*, and scores of others.

Wardour Street, noted for its old furniture and curiosity shops, would bring us into the heart of the **Soho** quarter, almost entirely occupied by foreigners of various nationalities. At the north-west angle of **Soho Square** is the **French Protestant**

LANCASTER GATE: The original station was opened on 30 July 1900 by the Central London Railway, again designed by Harry Bell Measures. The frontage is seen here in May 1955; it was demolished in 1965 and a new surface building constructed as part of the Park Gate Hotel.

The station today is fairly quiet, as the area lacks shops, bars or restaurants despite being close to central London. The station has only ever provided a lift service, with two lifts out of four in operation. It was closed for refurbishment from 3 July until 13 November 2006, and the new exterior is seen on 14 March 2007. *London Transport Museum/RG*

QUEENSWAY station opened on 30 July 1900 as 'Queen's Road', and was renamed Queensway on 9 September 1946. It was closed between 8 May 2005 and 14 June 2006 for modernisation works, part of which involved replacement of the station's lifts, which had been breaking down quite frequently, causing station closure or passengers having to walk up the long winding emergency stairs to exit the station.

Metronet, the private maintenance contractor, did a splendid job, although the deadline for opening was supposed to have been 9 May 2006. This caused some stir, but at least London Underground can feel proud of its newly refurbished station, especially the platforms, which look better and much brighter. *London Transport Museum/RG*

NOTTING HILL GATE: The last stage of construction of the Central London Railway is seen here on 5 August 1898. Without modern machinery the work was hard for the gangs of workers who built our 19th-century tube system. Note the temporary wooden platform structure and the tunnel ceiling and walls covered with white tiles.

Today the station is an interchange for the District and Circle lines, and every year the Notting Hill Carnival brings thousands of passengers here, although it is busy anyway, especially in the peak hours. The station must be due for refurbishment – paint is starting to peel from the tunnel walls. *London Transport Museum/RG*

HOLLAND PARK: The 'past' photograph was taken in 1914 and shows a typical Harry Bell Measures design. The building was refurbished in the 1990s – note that the side entrance has been replaced by a large window and the front entrance altered, with an extra window beside it. The station is provided with lifts to the platforms. *London Transport Museum/RG*

SHEPHERD'S BUSH: When this station opened in June 1900 it was the western terminus of the Central London Railway. You will find on the London Underground map that there are two stations named Shepherd's Bush, one on the Hammersmith & City Line and the other on the Central Line, and they are walking distance apart. At some stations, such as Hainault, the white enamel boards listing the stations show 'Shepherd's Bush Green' instead of 'Shepherd's Bush' – perhaps that was intended to be the name of the Central Line station, which would have been better in the long run. The 'past' photograph, taken in April 1935, shows the 'tombstone' sign and roundel on top of the building and a typical tobacconist's shop beside the entrance.

It was difficult to get a close shot of the station today because of the traffic lights and railings that fenced off the busy road. *London Transport Museum/RG*

BETWEEN SHEPHERD'S BUSH AND WHITE CITY: On the approach to White City from Shepherd's Bush (westbound), the track ran beside the old disused loop line at Wood Lane depot, the trackbed of which can be seen on the left. The first photograph was taken in 1992 from a train emerging from the tunnel, while the overhead view was taken in the summer of 2005.

With the closure of Wood Lane depot a new development is being built, and this section of track has been covered to allow buildings to be erected above. *All RG*

WOOD LANE DEPOT: With the opening of the Franco-British Exhibition of 1908 adjacent to the depot, the line was extended northwards to accommodate passengers to the exhibition. This extension took the form of a run-round loop with platforms, and it was extended again in 1917 to allow a further two platforms to be added. When Central Line services began to operate to Ealing Broadway in August 1920, the station was reconfigured to allow through running to Ealing from the City.

The first photograph shows one of the exhibition buildings that stood on stilts and was recently demolished. The second shows the grand Central London Railway power station, that won't be demolished. The third, dating from the 1970s, provides a reminder of how car sheds looked until recently, and sadly the final photograph shows the sheds being gradually demolished in 2006. The last train from the sidings ran on 5 January 2007. *RG (2)/ A. Richards/RG*

53

NEW WOOD LANE SIDINGS: During 2006 the eastbound platform at Wood Lane was completely demolished and the station was enclosed in a tunnel section until work began to transform the new sidings on the left-hand side of the 'past' photograph.

The new sub-surface 16-road sidings are the first of their size in the UK and were designed to allow the new development to be built above. The sidings also provide mess room, shower rooms and two floors of modern office accommodation, which train drivers will share with Metronet staff. *A. Rawling/RG*

WHITE CITY TRAINING CENTRE: For many years this training centre was used by all grades of London Underground staff and British Transport Police. It had many classrooms and offices; one room contained a mock-up platform, and another had train equipment for train crews to learn, rather than just reading from diagrams. The Rules & Regulations room had an actual train-set to show staff how signals worked. Behind the canteen was a large hall, often hired by the nearby BBC for filming programmes such as *Doctor Who* and *Z Cars*.

The training centre was demolished in 2006 to make room for the new development at Wood Lane as part of the depot. *Both RG*

WHITE CITY: I was pleased that I took this photograph of the old Wood Lane station in June 2002, not realising at the time that the building was going to be pulled down in the next few years. The station had closed in 1947 and gradually became neglected over the years and a target for graffiti artists and illegal bill-posters. It has been taken down brick by brick and will be rebuilt at Acton Museum.

Further up Wood Lane, the present-day White City station opened on 23 November 1947, replacing Wood Lane station. Although work had begun in 1938, to be completed by 1940, the war years delayed its opening. *Both RG*

EAST ACTON: This unique station opened in 1920 on the western extension from White City to Ealing Broadway. The platforms have wooden shelters rather than waiting rooms. This 1975 view of the westbound platform, showing a train of 1962 stock arriving, clearly shows how high above ground level the platforms were built, with steep sheltered stairs leading to the booking hall and entrance.

The station has recently been refurbished, but still retains its period look and wooden shelters. *J. Glover/RG*

NORTH ACTON was opened in 1923 with only two platforms on the line to Ealing Broadway, then from 1947 the service to West Ruislip was introduced, as shown in the 'past' photograph taken on 31 October 1977.

In 1992/93 a third track was laid, making the original eastbound track the middle line for reversing trains, with an island platform allowing trains to run in either direction. This area was re-signalled to allow such train moves, so the latest timetable includes more North Acton reverses. *J. Glover/RG*

NORTH ACTON JUNCTION was built in 1947 alongside the Great Western Railway (GWR) line to West Ruislip and beyond (on the right). The 'past' photograph, taken on 3 October 1977, shows trains of 1962 stock – the one on the left is running westbound towards West Ruislip, and that on the right is eastbound from West Ruislip to North Acton. The other two tracks swing away to the left towards Ealing Broadway.

The junction has hardly changed in 30 years, except that the signal cabin was closed in the late 1980s/early 1990s when all signals and points were worked from White City signal cabin. The train of 1992 stock has come from Ealing Broadway. *John Glover/RG*

This page WEST ACTON opened in 1923, and was the last station before Ealing Broadway; it is fairly quiet compared with the branch terminus. The station building is on the road bridge, as shown in the first photograph.

Between Ealing Broadway and West Acton the embankment vegetation was cut back on both sides a few years ago, to clear shrubs and trees and give it a new lease of life after many untouched years. The second photograph was taken on 10 May 1978 from the road bridge and the third was taken from a driving cab, travelling in the opposite direction. *RG/J. Glover/RG*

Opposite page EALING BROADWAY: The Great Western Railway opened its first section of line through Ealing Broadway on 6 April 1838, although the station did not open until 1 December, initially named Ealing. The Metropolitan District Railway (MDR), now the District Line, commenced services on 1 July 1879 when it opened its branch from Turnham Green. The Central London Railway arrived next, extending its tracks the short distance from its terminus at Wood Lane to meet the GWR line. CLR services began on 3 August 1920, with just one intermediate stop at East Acton.

In 1970 the GWR station building was demolished and replaced by a low concrete structure containing a ticket hall and shops. The high-rise office building has subsequently changed since the 'past' photograph, which dates from the 1980s. On the left is the former GWR line, while to the right of the Central Line are the District Line tracks. This is a very busy station with nine platforms. *J. Wright/RG*

HANGER LANE: The original station here was a halt on the Great Western Railway line to High Wycombe. Initially named Park Royal, it was changed when the nearby Piccadilly Line station of that name was opened in 1931. The building of Hanger Lane station and the rest of the line to West Ruislip was supervised by the GWR, using electrified tracks laid alongside its own. The line opened on 30 June 1947, with Hanger Lane station still incomplete; the 'past' photograph was taken on 25 November 1948, with the building nearing completion and surrounded by a wooden fence.

This distinctive building has been altered over the years without losing its appeal, as seen from the 'present' photograph. *London Transport Museum/RG*

PERIVALE: Again, the GWR had a Perivale Halt here, which opened on 2 May 1904 and closed when the Central Line station opened in 1947, as plain Perivale. The 'past' photograph, taken on 16 May 1955, shows a typical scene of a 'passimeter' booking office and the ticket collector sitting in her wooden box, ensuring that passengers had tickets for their journeys and collecting them from passengers on their way out of the station.

The 'present' photograph shows the modern automatic gates – gone are the days of ticket collectors on the Underground. Station Assistants stand near the automatic gates to ensure that everything runs smoothly and to allow passengers with heavy luggage or pushchairs to use the gate beside the barriers. *London Transport Museum/RG*

GREENFORD: The original station on the main line was opened by the GWR on 1 October 1904. The Second World War held up work on the Central Line extension, built under the LPTB's 1935-40 'New Works Programme', resulting in an opening on 30 June 1947. The 'past' photograph, taken on 19 March 1982, shows a train of 1962 stock departing from the eastbound platform, while a Class 121 DMU arrives.

The 'present' photograph, taken on 19 December 1998, clearly shows that the tube train has changed to the 1992 stock and the DMU to a First Great Western Class 165. The centre bay platform is used by First Great Western for its shuttle service to Paddington via West Ealing.

Greenford once had a siding for reversing, but Northolt, the next station along the line (see page 6), became busier, serving RAF Northolt, and it was decided that it would be better to reverse trains there instead. The reversing siding is still used on a regular basis, especially during the peak hours; trains can also reverse back east from the westbound platform if needed. *Both John Glover*

SOUTH RUISLIP station opened on 21 November 1948 with the completion of the Central Line extension from London into Buckinghamshire after the Second World War. It was decided that the line would terminate at West Ruislip, not Denham as first planned, because of 'green belt' legislation. The past photograph, taken on 16 May 1955, shows the old booking hall.

Beyond Northolt Junction the Central Line tracks run on the former Great Western & Great Central Joint line, now the Chiltern Line from Marylebone towards High Wycombe. South Ruislip station was closed in February 2006 for refurbishment work when brown asbestos was discovered, and re-opened shortly after the work was carried out. The 'present' photograph shows the difference. *London Transport Museum/RG*

RUISLIP GARDENS: Main-line services stopped calling at Ruislip Gardens in 1958 and the station closed, leaving only the Central Line. The station has an island platform and some trains terminate here to enter the depot rather than at West Ruislip, although more enter the depot from the latter station, otherwise they miss the train-wash. This photograph of the temporary booking hall was taken on 16 May 1955 (the station was not finally completed until 1961) and clearly shows both BR and London Transport logos on the 'Trains' sign.

Today the booking hall looks very different, following the rebuilding of the booking hall and recent modernisation. *London Transport Museum/RG*

WEST RUISLIP is the end of the line, although the station was not designed as a terminus because the line was intended to continue to Denham before that proposal was scrapped. If the extension had been constructed the next station would have been Harefield Road.

The 'past' photograph, taken in January, 1990 shows 1962 stock in both platforms. The driver and guard normally closed the doors on the first carriage to keep the heat in, the heating in the trains being very poor in those days. Guards were ordered to turn off the carriage heating in the tube tunnels because of the fire risk, and by the time they arrived at the open sections the heating took time to get warm again.

Today the station has been refurbished with better lighting, CCTV cameras, an improved public address system and safety equipment. Note the yellow lines painted on the platform – these were introduced on every Underground station for safety reasons, passengers being advised to stand behind them.

The Central Line tracks continue for a short distance beyond the station before ending at red stop lights, as shown in the third photograph. *D. Henderson/RG (2)*

WEST RUISLIP: At every terminating station the driver and guard had to change the destination blind at each end of the train by turning a small handle inside the cab. To check the indication, some train crews found it more convenient to lean out of the front cab door, rather than look through the small window at the bottom of the destination blind inside the cab, as seen in the photograph taken on 9 February 1980.

With the modern 1992 stock the driver has to enter a number code in the keypad – for example '01' for West Ruislip, or '46' for Epping. Note that the Chiltern Line platforms are served by a separate station building.
J. Glover/RG

WOODFORD TO HAINAULT

This page WOODFORD station has certainly seen its fair share of tube stock in its time, especially in the mid-1960s. While the 1962 tube stock was busy in service – running from Epping to West Ruislip and Ealing Broadway, as seen in the first photograph, the Craven and 1967 stock were still carrying out their trails for the Victoria Line (second view). Station staff had to assist in detraining at Woodford before the Craven and 1967 tube stock reversed into the siding, which is now a run-round loop although still used as a siding for reversing trains. A train of 1992 stock enters the refurbished station in the third view. *David Henderson/J. Wright/RG*

Opposite page RODING VALLEY is served by Central Line trains running between Woodford and Hainault, with some services continuing onwards via Newbury Park to West Ruislip and Ealing Broadway. This route was originally part of a Great Eastern Railway line from Woodford to Ilford, which opened on 1 May 1903, and a Roding Valley Halt was opened by the London & North Eastern Railway, successor to the GER, on 3 February 1936 as a result of new housing developments between Buckhurst Hill and Woodford. As part of the LPTB's 1935-40 'New Works Programme' the majority of the 'Fairlop loop' was transferred to form the eastern extension of the Central Line. Work commenced in 1938 but was suspended with the outbreak of war in 1939; it was not completed until 1948. The halt closed on 29 November 1947, to re-open on 21 November 1948 as a London Underground station. The first photograph shows a train of 1962 tube stock approaching the station on 1 March 1982.

Roding Valley station is one of the most lightly used on the Underground and was unmanned for many years, although equipped with CCTV cameras for security. However, it was refurbished in 2006 and, with the introduction of the new Central Line timetable on 19 November of that year, it became manned once again. A train of 1992 stock approaches the station, and is working fully automatically. *J. Glover/ RG*

CHIGWELL: This station's long platforms served steam trains to Ilford from 1903. By the mid-1960s 1967 tube stock was being used to test ATO (automatic train operation) for the Victoria Line, together with the 1960 tube stock, which was also adapted for ATO.

For many years this station closed at 8.00pm because of light passenger use, but since 19 November 2006 it has remained open until the close of traffic. The 'present' picture shows 1992 tube stock, running fully automatically with new automatic equipment since 1994, one of many vast changes in today's railway technology. *J. Wright/RG*

GRANGE HILL is located between Chigwell and Hainault, and the original GER/LNER facility closed from 29 November 1947 to re-open on 21 November 1948 as a Central Line station. The station booking hall was reconstructed following destruction by a Second World War bomb. Trains can enter Hainault depot from both platforms here, via the train-wash road. This photograph shows a train of 1962 stock on the 'outer rail' (westbound line) in the 1970s.

Despite a new station canopy and refurbishment, the station has still kept its original appearance throughout the years with its old waiting rooms and station staff offices. A train of 1992 stock waiting for the signal to clear before it continues its journey to Hainault. *J. Wright/RG*

HAINAULT DEPOT was built in 1939, and has seen many changes over the years. The US Army Transportation Corps used the depot in the war years until 1945, when London Transport took it over from 14 December. The depot carries out maintenance on its fleet of 85 trains, and was the first depot on the Underground to benefit from new-technology carriage-cleaning equipment. The depot can stable at least 220 carriages in its north and south depot roads and sheds. The 'past' photograph was taken from the signal cabin in the 1970s and shows 1962 stock.

Today 1992 stock has taken the place of the earlier trains, but the only track alteration is the wash road on the extreme right; drivers go through the train-wash to the north neck, then reverse and stable on one of the depot roads. This photograph was taken at ground level, as the signal cabin is now closed. *J. Wright/RG*

HAINAULT TO LEYTONSTONE

HAINAULT station was opened on 1 May 1903 on the Great Eastern Railway's Woodford to Ilford branch. Due to lack of custom it closed to passenger traffic from 1 October 1908, but re-opened on 2 March 1930. Steam trains were suspended on 29 November 1947, and electrified Central Line passenger services to central London via Gants Hill commenced on 31 May 1948. Alterations at Hainault included a new island platform, allowing the station to handle the bulk of terminating trains and provide access to Hainault depot. The 'past' photograph taken in the 1970s and shows a train of 1962 tube stock in Platform 2.

By 1999 a new staff building had been built, providing staff with modern facilities at long last rather than being cramped in the previous train crew room on Platform 1. The recent photograph shows the staff-only footbridge that gives access from both platforms to the new building. *J. Wright/RG*

HAINAULT: Train drivers at Hainault had their own rota system for the line – they were mainly long-service drivers who preferred just to operate on this line, allowing them a break from the tunnel work they had experienced for many years. As a guard in my younger days I remember that they used to have their own table in the mess room and you dared not sit with them unless you were invited. A train of 1967 tube stock – being tested for automatic working on the Hainault to Woodford Line prior to the opening of the Victoria Line in 1968 – stands on the right in Platform 2 beside a train of 1962 tube stock in Platform 1, waiting to continue its journey to Ealing Broadway.

I could not resist taking this night shot at Hainault with trains of 1992 tube stock side by side. In December 2006 the station was undergoing refurbishment, hence the scaffolding erected on the station platform and canopy. *J. Wright/RG*

FAIRLOP station is only a short distance – 0.76km – from Hainault and has very light passenger use, with a small booking hall and office at a lower level. A train of 1962 stock arrives at the station on 18 March 1982, using the long platforms that were once served by GER steam trains.

By 2006 the station had been fully refurbished, but still shows signs of its Edwardian origin, including canopies that bear the 'GER' monogram in their brackets. *J. Glover/RG*

BARKINGSIDE also opened with the line on 1 May 1903, and its GER/LNER buildings are Grade II listed. The station was temporarily closed to passenger traffic during the First World War, from 22 May 1916 until 30 June 1919. Steam trains were suspended on 29 November 1947 and the newly electrified route to central London via Gants Hill opened on 31 May 1948. From 14 December 1947 only empty train movements had been allowed from Newbury Park to the new depot at Hainault.

The elegant Edwardian station, with its small bell tower and cupola, has not change very much since the 'past' photograph was taken on 21 February 1953. The 'present' photograph I took looking in the opposite direction to show the features more clearly. *London Transport Museum/RG*

NEWBURY PARK: A train of 1962 stock approaches Newbury Park station in July 1990, passing the siding that was once the GER/LNER line to Ilford from Temple Mills Yard via Woodford.

The track and points were taken out of use some years later, leaving just an empty piece of land today, as a train of 1992 tube stock leaves the tunnel section to continue its journey to Hainault. *John Glover/RG*

NEWBURY PARK has the same history as Barkingside, except that it was a temporary terminus until 31 May 1948. Even today some trains terminate here, as booked in the working timetable. The station booking hall is on a higher level from the two platforms – the 'past' photograph, taken on 28 October 1953, shows the wooden ticket collector's box and iron railings, a typical scene on the London Underground before automatic barriers were introduced.

Today the automatic barriers and Oyster cards make the passenger flow quicker and more convenient, especially in the peak hours. *London Transport Museum/RG*

GANTS HILL: Construction of the line began in the 1930s but was suspended during the Second World War, the tunnels being used as an air-raid shelter and munitions factory. The station finally opened on 14 December 1947, built beneath Gants Hill roundabout and accessed via a pedestrian subway. The silhouette-type roundel displays 'London Transport' in the 'past' photograph taken on 29 October 1953, now changed to 'Underground'. *London Transport Museum/RG*

REDBRIDGE: Renowned tube architect Charles Holden designed this and the other station buildings on the line. Redbridge is the shallowest station on the network, being only 7.9 metres (26 feet) beneath the surface. The station opened on 4 December 1947, having been delayed by the onset of the Second World War, during which the Plessey company established an aircraft parts factory in the tunnels. The second photograph shows the island platform with its matrix display and fluorescent lighting. *Both RG*

WANSTEAD station has certainly seen some changes over the years. The ceiling of the tunnel sections was removed in the 1990s because of asbestos, which was sealed to make it safe; this revealed its concrete and iron structure, and made the station look very dismal with its yellow tiles. The station is currently being refurbished to high standards with better lighting. The next station continuing westbound is Leytonstone. *Both RG*

CENTRAL LINE ROLLING-STOCK

Four types of rolling-stock are currently used on the Central Line, each one serving a particular purpose. Today's 1992 tube stock, seen in the first picture, is fully automatic, and replaced the 1962 tube stock from 1994. These trains were designed with large driving cabs and wider doors on the carriages.

Only a few remaining units of the 1962 stock remain after the majority of the fleet was scrapped from 1994. A familiar sight in the leaf-fall season is a train of 1962 stock converted to a 'Sandite' train (*below*), which sprays a mixture of sand, gel and metal filings onto the track to prevent wheelslip. This train had to be fitted with ATP equipment because of the new signalling system on the Central Line.

Of the 1960 tube stock (Cravens) only a few examples remain (*above*). This one was converted into a 'Track Recording Train' and is used everywhere on the Underground for its main purpose. Again, it had to be fitted with ATP equipment.

Ballast locomotives (*below*) are a common sight on the Central Line, especially with all the new track replacement work taking place on sections of the line. Only a few locomotives from the fleet have been equipped with ATP equipment to serve on the Central Line, and these are stabled at West Ruislip or Lillie Bridge depots. *All RG*

The interior of tube stock past and present has certainly changed over the years. These two pictures compare the 1962 and 1992 stock. Although the 1962 seating was more comfortable, standing room was very limited. The 1992 doorways are wider to allow faster boarding and alighting at busy stations, especially in the peak hours; there are also wider windows and better-designed hand-grips. The 1992 stock was also fitted with armrests until troublesome youths began to remove them – London Underground decided to remove the remainder, as the cost of replacing them would have been extremely high. Fire extinguishers suffered the same fate and are now only located in the driving cabs. *A. Richards/RG*

Driving cabs have also changed with the advent of modern technology, providing the driver with a larger cab and a comfortable seat that can be altered to suit the individual's driving position. The 1962 stock had a master controller (the 'dead man's handle') for forward movement and a separate brake handle; the speed monitor was above the pressure gauge for the main and train air line, which was above the brake handle, with the train whistle button just below the pressure gauge. The driver had to insert a control key in the barrel behind him and use his reverser key (a spanner-type key) for forward and reverse movements; he also had to change the head and tail lights and the destination blind before commencing each journey.

The 1992 stock has made life easier and working conditions better for the driver. The seat is more comfortable and the traction brake controller (TBC) controls movement and braking all in one. The CCTV monitor and door control buttons have replaced those operated by the guard, and the train runs fully automatically. *Both RG*

In March 1983 three four-car trains were ordered, and were displayed at Woodford in June 1987, with staff and passengers asked to indicate their preferences regarding their design and features. Each train was made by a different manufacture and was a different colour – red, blue and green. Eventually, in September 1989 an order for 85 eight-car trains was placed with BREL (later taken over by ABB), with 20 further cars ordered for the Waterloo & City Line. This stock is known as the 1992 stock and each train weighed 32 tons less than the 1962 stock it replaced on the Central line.

These two photographs show the other proposed trains, photographed on the Jubilee Line in May 1988 where they ran a passenger service until one of them became derailed north of Neasden station on 14 August 1989. One of the trains is on display at the Acton Museum and the other two were scrapped. *J. Wright/RG*

CENTRAL LINE SIGNALLING

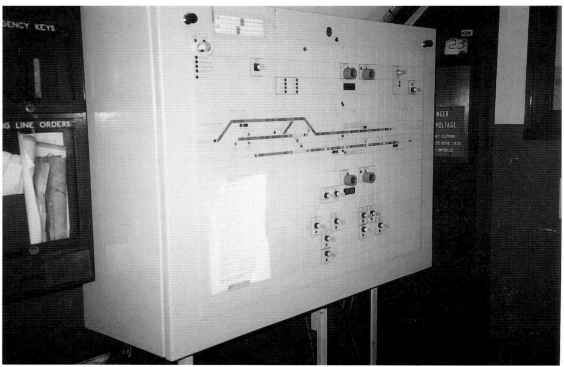

Who needs signal cabins and hundreds of colour light signals to operate a railway? The Central Line doesn't, thanks to ATP (automatic train protection) and ATO (automatic train operation) working. The Control Centre at Wood Lane has replaced at least 13 signal cabins since 1994, including the typical LT example at Loughton (*left*). If signalling problems arise at Wood Lane, local control can be introduced at controlled stations by using emergency control panels, which are located either in the signal cabins or station rooms; the one illustrated (*below left*) is in the disused signal cabin at Holborn. They are also located at depots for shunting moves, etc.

The Central Line still has colour light signals (*above*), mostly in controlled areas where points are involved and as station starter signals, but block marker boards (*below*) have replaced them between stations. These do not indicate if it is safe to pass them, like colour light signals, but with ATP the driver's target speed remains at line speed as long as the section ahead is clear – if it is not, the target speed drops to zero, indicating that the driver must stop at the next block marker board ahead. When the train is running in automatic mode, it will stop automatically and depart when the section ahead is clear. When driving in coded manual mode the driver hears an audible signal in the cab to tell him whether the signal ahead is clear or at danger. *All RG*

INDEX OF LOCATIONS